HOW TO OBTAIN FUNDING FOR YOUR START-UP AND LOANS FOR YOUR BUSINESS

L.C. Green, Jr.

HOW TO OBTAIN FUNDING FOR YOUR START-UP AND LOANS FOR YOUR BUSINESS

LIMITS OF LIABILITY AND DISCLAIMER OR WARRANTY:
This publication is designed to provide information and education in regard to the subject matter covered. It is sold with the understanding that the author and publishers are not engaged in rendering legal, accounting or other professional services. If legal advice or other expert assistance is required, please seek the services of a competent professional person.

ISBN: 9781530726974

PUBLISHED BY
LC GREEN & ASSOCIATES, INC.
(310) 515-7316

www.lcgreen.com
Email: info@lcgreenjr.com
www.lcwriter.com
www.facebook.com/lcgreenbooksforsuccess

ABOUT THE AUTHOR

LC Green & Associates
"Business of the Year," Constant Contact 2013

LC Green, Jr. is a Best-selling Author

Founder of **LC Green & Associates, Inc.**, a financial management firm, **LC Green, Jr.** has been in the accounting and financial management fields for more than Thirty years.

As an instructor at five Los Angeles County colleges for over ten years, Mr. Green teaches Accounting, Bookkeeping, Taxation and related Financial Management courses. Mr. Green *also* teaches continuing education for insurance and tax professionals and conducts workshops nationwide for major corporations and non-profit organizations,

LC Green, Jr. has delivered more than one hundred fifty speeches to diverse audiences throughout the west coast, with emphasis on business and personal financial management. *And* Mr. Green is an administrator with the Internal Revenue Service's Taxpayer Assistance Program, and the State of California's Tax Preparer's Program.

He sets up Investment Clubs and is a member of two investment clubs. He knows and understand investments.

LC Green, Jr. has authored many helpful articles for various magazines, books and newsletters and has coauthored several books with author such as Dr. Rosie Milligan, Dr. George Fraser and Les Brown. His books *include*:

- *Mission Unstoppable*, Coauthor

- *Steps to Success*

- *A Blueprint for Business Success*

- *How to Avoid / Survive an Audit*

- *How to Use Traditional Marketing Principles in an online Marketing World*

- *The Principals of Small Business Taxes*

- *The Principals of Financial Control*

TABLE OF CONTENTS

INTRODUCTION

Joe S. opened a small corner café with its main product being smoothies and yogurt. His goal was to be a smaller version of Jamba Juice. He even envisioned having a franchise of his healthy drink cafés. Everything started out perfect. The stainless steel fountains were glistening, the various fruit drinks were colorful, and the blenders were as pristine clear as glass. However, one year later, Joe's newfound customers went to the location and found that the café was closed. So what happened?

Do you think Joe intended for his small business to fail?

How many times have you seen small businesses open, then close within the first year? Unfortunately, this is not unusual. In Forbes magazine, "According to Bloomberg, 8 out of 10 entrepreneurs who start businesses fail within the first 18 months. A whopping 80% crash and burn." http://onforb.es/1QPDFyR

As a small business owner, yourself, do you worry if you will be able to keep your doors open? Have you ever wondered how you could keep your cash flow going, or if you were going to be able to start or stay in business at all?

What is the number one reason for businesses failing?

The number one reason businesses fail is because the businesses did not have a well thought-out plan. As the saying goes, if you fail to plan, then you plan to fail. So how can you keep from becoming a statistic? You can plan to arm yourself with needed information as to how to get money for your business.

Let's examine the source of the problem. The biggest reason for business failure is generally because of a lack of funding and a shortage of cash flow.

How you fund your business will have a lot to do with your successful outcome. So in the next chapters, we will look at a number of different ways to fund a small business.

CHAPTER ONE

Where Should you Begin?

Obtaining Capital

The first place to start is with your local bank. In this chapter, you will learn ways you can get much needed capital from the bank.

To begin with, many new business owners are so excited to open their first business account, they overlook one important step. That one *Big* mistake small business owners often make is not talking with the bank's business officer. Yes, it is a good business practice to talk with the bank's business office before opening your business account. Talking with the business officer gives you the opportunity to know want kind of funding the bank offers.

The ability to obtain money when you need it is as necessary to the operation of your business as is a good location, the right equipment, reliable sources of supplies and materials, or an adequate labor force. Before a bank or any other lending agency will lend you money, the loan officer must feel satisfied with the answers to the five following questions:

- What sort of person are you, the prospective borrower? By all odds, the character of the borrower comes first.

- Next, is your ability to manage your business.

- What are you going to do with the money? The answer to this question will determine the type of loan—short or long-term. Money to be used for the purchase of purchase of seasonal inventory will require quicker repayment than money used to buy fixed assets.

- When and how do you plan to pay it back? Your banker's judgment of your business ability and the type of loan will be a deciding factor in the answer to the question.

- Is the cushion in the loan large enough? In other words, does the amount requested make suitable allowance for unexpected developments? The banker decides this question on the basis of your financial statement that sets forth the condition of your business and on the collateral pledged.

Finally, what is the outlook for business in general, and for your business, in particular?

Why Adequate Financial Data Is A "Must"

In the same way you want to get a loan, the banker wants to make loans to businesses that are solvent, profitable, and growing.

However, there are two basic financial statements used to determine those conditions. They are the balance sheet and profit and loss statement. The former is the major yardstick for solvency and the latter for profits. A continuous series of these two statements over a period of time is the principal device for measuring financial stability and growth potential.

In interviewing loan applicants and in studying their records, the banker is especially interested in the following facts and figures:

General Information:

- First, are the books and records up-to-date and in good condition? What is the condition of accounts payable? Of notes payable? What are the salaries of the owner-manager and other company officers? Are all taxes being paid? What is the order backlog? How many employees? What is the insurance coverage?

- *Accounts Receivable*: Are there indications that some of the accounts receivable have already been pledged to another creditor? What is the accounts receivable turnover?

- Is the account receivable total weakened because many customers are far behind in their payments? Has a large enough reserve been set up to cover doubtful accounts? How much do the largest accounts owe and what percentage of your total accounts does this amount represent?

- *Inventories*: Is merchandise in good shape or will it have to be marked down? How much raw material is on hand?

How much work is in process? How much of the inventory is finished goods?

- Is there any obsolete inventory? Has an excessive amount of inventory been consigned to customers? Is inventory turnover in line with the turnover for other businesses in the same industry? Is money being tied up too long in inventory?

- *Fixed Assets*: What is the type, age, and condition of the equipment? What are the depreciation policies? What are the details of mortgages or conditional sales contracts? What are the future acquisition plans?

In summary, you want to have your paper work together. Action steps:

1. Ask for a meeting with a business loan officer before you open your account.

2. Have your business statements together, such as your balance sheet and profit and loss statement.

3. Take an inventory of all your assets.

CHAPTER TWO

What Kind of Money Will You Need?

When you set out to borrow money for your firm, it is important to know the kind of money you need from a bank or other lending institution. There are three kinds of money loans: short term, long-term money, and equity capital.

The purpose for which the funds are to be used is an important factor in deciding the kind of money needed. But even so, deciding what kind of money to use is not always easy.

It is sometimes complicated by the fact that you may be using some of the various kinds of money at the same time and for identical purposes.

Keep in mind that a very important distinction among the types of money is the source of repayment. Generally, short-term loans are repaid from the liquidation of current assets that they have financed. Long-term loans are usually repaid from earnings.

What are the different type of bank loans?

Short-Term Bank Loans

You can use short-term bank loans for purposes such as financing accounts receivable for, say 30 to 60 days. Or you can use them for purposes that take longer to pay off—such as for building a seasonal inventory over a period of 5 to 6 months. Usually, lenders expect short-term loans to be repaid after their purposes have been served, for example, accounts have been paid by the borrower's customers, and inventory loans, when the inventory has been converted into Salable merchandises.

Banks lend money either on your general credit reputation with an unsecured loan or on a secured loan.

The Unsecured Loan is the most frequently used form of bank credit for short- term purposes. You do not have to put up collateral because the bank relies on your credit reputation.

The Secured Loan involves a pledge of some or all of your assets. The bank requires security as a protection for its depositors against the risks that are involved even in business situations where the chances of success are good.

Term Borrowing

Term borrowing provides money you plan to pay back over a fairly long time. Some people break it down into two forms: (1) Intermediate-loans longer than one year but fewer than five years, and (2) long-term-loans for more than five years.

However, for your purpose of matching the kind of money to the needs of your company, think of term borrowing as a kind of money that you probably will pay back in periodic installments from lendings.

What Is Equity Capital?

Some people confuse term borrowing and equity (or investment) capital. Yet there is a big difference. You don't have to repay equity money. It is money you get by selling a part interest in your business.

You take people into your company who are willing to risk their money in it. They are interested in potential income rather than in an immediate return on their investment. This is different than money you borrow from the bank. The investor will get a percent of your business as repayment.

Action Steps:

1.   Decide what kind of loan you want.

2.   Consider if you would prefer to have an investor own a percent of your business as repayment.

3.   Evaluate if you need the business loan for a short term or long term.

CHAPTER THREE

How Much Money Should You Borrow?

The amount of money you need to borrow depends on why you need funding. Figuring the amount of money required for business construction, conversion, or expansion—term loans, or equity capital—is relatively easy. Equipment manufactures, architects, and builders will readily supply you with cost estimates. On the other hand, the amount of working capital you need depends upon the type of business you're in. While rule-of- thumb ratios may be helpful as a starting point, a detailed projection of sources and uses of funds over some future period of time, usually for twelve months, is a better approach. In this way, the characteristics of the particular situation can be taken into account. Such a projection is developed through the combination of a predicted budget and a cash forecast.

The budget is based on recent operating experience plus your best judgment of performance during the coming period. The cash forecast is your estimate of cash receipts and disbursements during the budget period. Thus, the budget and cash forecast together represent your plan for meeting your working capital requirements.

In summary, to plan your working capital requirements, it is important to know the "cash flow" your business will generate. This involves simply considering all cash receipts and disbursements as they occur. These elements are listed in a profit and loss statement adapted to show cash flow. They should be projected for each month.

Action Steps:

1. Do a projected cash forecast and disbursements, which will predict your intake for the next year.

2. Put together a 12-month profit and loss statement of all cash receipts and disbursements as they occur.

3. Show your current balance sheet.

4. Do a start-up work sheet.

CHAPTER FOUR

What Kind of Collateral Should You Use?

Sometimes your signature is the only security the bank needs when making you a loan. Other times, the bank requires additional assurance that the money will be repaid. The kind and amount of security depends on the bank and on the borrower's situation.

If the loan required cannot be justified by the borrower's financial statements alone, a pledge of security may bridge the gap. The types of security are: endorsers; co-makers and guarantors; assignment of leases; trust receipts and floor planning; chattel mortgages; real estate; accounts receivable; savings accounts; life insurance policies; stocks and bonds.

In a substantial number of states where the Uniform Commercial Code has been enacted, paperwork for recording loan transactions will be greatly simplified a loan.

Endorsers, Co-Makers and Guarantors

Borrowers often get other people to sign a note in order to bolster their own credit. These endorsers are continentally liable for the note they sign. If the borrower fails to pay up, the bank expects the endorser to make the note good. Sometimes, the endorser may be asked to pledge assets or securities, too.

A Co-Maker (Or co-signer) is one who creates an obligation jointly with the borrower. In such cases, the bank can collect directly from either the maker or the co-maker.

A Guarantor is one who guarantees the payment of a note by signing a guaranty commitment. Both private and government lenders often require guarantees from officers of corporations in order to assure continuity of effective management.

Sometimes, a manufacturer will act as guarantor for customers.

Assignment of Leases

The assigned lease as security is similar to the guarantee, franchise situations.

It is used, for example, in cases like these. The bank lends the money on a building and takes a mortgage. Then the lease, which the dealer and the parent franchise company work out, is assigned so that the bank automatically receives the rent payments. In this manner, the bank is guaranteed repayment of the loan.

Warehouse Receipts

Banks also take commodities as security by lending money on a warehouse receipt. Such a receipt is usually delivered directly to the bank and shows that the merchandise used as security either has been placed in a public warehouse or has been left on your premises under the control of one of your employees who is bonded (as in field warehousing). Such loans are generally made on staple or standard merchandise, which can be reality marketed. The typical warehouse receipt loan is for a percentage of the estimated value of the goods used as security.

Trust Receipts and Floor Planning

Some merchandise, such as automobiles, appliances, and boats, has to be displayed to be sold. The only way many small marketers can afford such displays is by borrowing money. Such loans are often secured by a note and a trust receipt.

This trust receipt is the legal paper for floor planning. It is used for serial-numbered merchandise. When you sign one, you (1) acknowledge receipt of the merchandise, (2) agree to keep the merchandise in trust for the bank, and (3) promise to pay the bank as you sell the goods.

Chattel Mortgages

If you buy equipment, such as a cash register or a delivery truck, you may want to get a chattel mortgage loan. You give the bank a lien on the equipment you are buying.

The bank also evaluates the present and future market value of the equipment being used to secure the loan. How rapidly will it depreciate? Does the borrower have the necessary fare, theft, property damage, and public liability insurance on the equipment? The banker has to be sure that the borrower protects the equipment.

Real Estate

Real estate is another form of collateral for long-term loans. When taking a real estate mortgage, the bank finds out: (1) the location of the real estate, (2) its physical condition, (3) its foreclosure value, and (4) the amount of insurance carried on the property.

Accounts Receivable

Many banks lend money on accounts receivable. In effect, you are counting on your customers to pay your note.

The bank may take accounts receivable on a notification or a non-notification plan. Under the notification plan, the purchaser of the goods is informed by the bank that his or her account has been assigned to it and he or she is asked to pay the bank. Under the non-notification plan, your customers continue to pay collateral.

Life Insurance

Another kind of collateral is life insurance. Banks will lend up to the cash value of a life insurance policy. You have to assign the policy to the bank.

21

Stocks And Bonds

If you use stocks and bonds as collateral, they must be marketable. As a protection against market declines and possible expenses of liquidation, banks usually lend no more than seventy-five percent of the market value of high-grade stock. On Federal government or municipal bonds, they may be willing to lend ninety percent or more of their market value.

In summary, there are many ways to put up collateral to ensure you will get the loan. You must count the costs, and weigh the risks for your individual circumstances.

CHAPTER FIVE

What Are the Lender's Rules?

L ending institutions are not just interested in loan repayments. They are also interested in borrowers with healthy profit-making businesses. Therefore, whether or not collateral is required for a loan, they set loan limitations and restrictions to protect themselves against unnecessary risk and at the same time against poor management practices by their borrowers.

Some owner-managers consider loan limitations a burden. Yet others feel that such limitations also offer an opportunity for improving their management techniques.

Especially with long-term loans, the borrower, as well as the lender, should be thinking of: (1) the net earning power of the borrower company, (2) the capability of its management,

(3) the long-range prospects of the company, and (4) the long-range prospects of the industry of which the company is a part. Such factors often mean that limitations increase as the duration of the loan increases.

What Kind of Limitations?

The kinds of limitations that an owner-manager finds sets upon the company depend to a great extent on the company. If the company is a good risk, only minimum limitations need be set. A poor risk, of course, is different. Its limitations should be greater than those of a stronger company.

Look now for a few moments at the kinds of limitations and restrictions, which the lender may set. Knowing what they are can help you see how they affect your operations.

The limitations that you will usually run into when you borrow money are:

- Repayment terms

- Pledging or the use of security

- Periodic reporting

Do's and Don'ts When Working With a Banker

- Make an appointment—don't just drop in.

- Make sure you have enough time and the banker has enough time to get the business done.

- Tell it like it is, both good and bad.

- Be prepared: bring all necessary information with you. Try to have exact figures on all expense items, if available, rather than estimates.

- Think things through before you make a request, and be certain to support your request.

- Learn to listen. The banker is a source of counsel and guidance.

- If you don't understand what has been said or not said, ask questions.

- Sell yourself and your abilities.

- If you have to wait, don't get impatient—don't leave.

- When going to the bank to seek a loan, have a definite plan but one that is flexible enough to allow for changes in operations.

- Don't make promises to your banker for interest rate quotations on a loan. Go into the bank and discuss it with the lending officer.

- Keep your banker informed of progress or problems. In other words, keep the communication channels open.

- If you fill out a personal financial statement, always complete the form thoroughly and truthfully.

Questions a Banker is Going to Ask You

What can you do to prepare yourself better when going to a banker for a loan? The following are some basic questions that a lending officer will ask you when you sit down and request a loan.

- What amount of money do you want?

- What is the purpose of the loan?

- What are the primary sources of repayment?

- What kind of collateral do you have to support your loan request?

- Do you have the services of an accountant?

- Do you have the services of an attorney?

- Do you have business life insurance?

- Do you have business protection insurance?

- How much do you, as a businessperson, know about your business?

- How much personal debt do you have?

- How much competition will you be faced with?

- How much money do you have to put into the business or have you already invested in the business?

So be prepared when you sit down with the banker. The next chapter will look at the loan package.

CHAPTER SIX

What is a Loan Package and How
Should You Prepare It?

This chapter will break down what you need to put in a loan package. The outline of a complete loan package below illustrates the type of detailed presentation sometimes required by lenders, including banks and the Small Business Administration. However, this degree of detail is often unnecessary for businesses already known to the lender.

SUMMARY
- Nature of the business
- Amount and purpose of loan
- Repayment terms
- Equity share of borrower (debt/equity ratio after loan)
- Security or collateral (listed with market value estimates and quotes on cost of equipment to be purchased with the loan proceeds)

Personal Information (On All Corporate Officers, Directors, and Any Individuals Owning 20 Percent or More of The Business)

- Education, work history, and business experience

- Credit references Income tax statements (last three years)

- Financial statement (not over 60 days old)

- Firm Information (Whichever Is Applicable Below—A, B, OR C)
  - New Business

  - Business

  - Life and casualty insurance coverage

  - Lease agreement Partnership, corporation or franchise papers, if applicable

- Business Acquisition (Buyout)
  - Information on acquisition

  - Business history (include seller's name, reasons for sale)

  - Current balance sheet (not over 60 days old)

  - Current profit and loss statements (preferably fewer than 60 days old)

  - Business' federal income tax returns (past three to five years)

- Cash flow statements for last year

- Copy of sales agreement with breakdown of inventory, fixtures, equipment, licenses, goodwill, and other costs

- Description and dates of permits already acquired

- Lease agreement if you operate a bricks-and-mortar business

- Business plan

- Life and casualty insurance

- Partnership, corporation, or franchise papers, inapplicable

- Existing Business Expansion
  - Information on existing business

  - Business history

  - Current balance sheet (not more than 60 days old)

  - Current profit and loss statements (not more than 60 days old)

  - Cash flow statements for past year

  - Federal income tax returns for past three to five years

  - Lease agreement and permit data

  - Business plan

- Life and casualty insurance

- Partnership, corporate, or franchise papers, inapplicable

- Projections
  - Profit and loss projection (monthly, for one year) and explanation of projections

  - Cash flow projection (monthly, for one year) and explanation of projections

  - Projected balance sheet (one year after loan) and explanation of projections

Sources of Capital
(Other than Banks and Commercial Lenders)

Personal Investment

Your first and most likely source of capital is, of course, yourself. The amount of money you decide to invest in starting a business will depend partly on how much money you have readily available, be it in savings, in investments, or paid into your home. It will also depend on how the ownership in the business is to be divided.

Your chances of avoiding investing any of your own money in the business are slim.

Since forming a business involves risk, prospective credi-
tors and investors will expect you, the owner, to share in that
risk. However, there are exceptions. If you have a unique idea
or valuable skills to contribute to the business, these might
augment capital or be an acceptable substitute for it. Many of
the technology giants such as Twitter, have gotten their intial
funding through investors. According to Wikepedia, "Twitter raised
over US $57 million from venture capitalist growth funding, although
exact numbers are not publicly disclosed. Twitter's first A round of funding was for an undisclosed amount that is rumored to have been between
US $1 million and US $5 million.[165] Its second B round of funding in 2008
was for US $22 million[166]and its third C round of funding in 2009 was
for US $35 million from Institutional Venture Partners and Benchmark
Capital along with an undisclosed amount from other investors including Union Square Ventures, Spark Capital, and Insight Venture Partners.
[165] Twitter is backed by Union Square Ventures, Digital Garage, Spark
Capital, and Bezos Expeditions.[167] Should you be planning to finance
your business solely from your own personal resources, on the
other hand, you may want to reconsider. Instead of putting the
money directly into the business, it would be to your advantage
to use it as collateral for a loan to the business. Not only would
this build up your credit standing, but, since the interest paid on
the loan is a tax-deductible expense, the loan would be virtually
cost-free.

You can try any or a combination of the above ideas to help
get a loan or investors on board to help fund your business.

CHAPTER SEVEN

How Can You Use Alternative Funding Sources?

Family and Friends

Obtaining money from family and friends, through loans or investments, may also be an alternative. But, bear in mind that this can strain both your personal and your business relationships unless the proper safeguards are taken.

The provisions for the repayment of such loans should be clearly stated in writing, including the duration of each loan, the interest rate, and the payment schedule. In this way, you can minimize future misunderstandings over the nature of the money entrusted to you.

When relatives or friend become investors in your business, the terms of this association should be stipulated in advance. How much of a say will they have in running the business? Do you have the right to buy back their interest in the company? How will the proceeds be distributed? All this should be put in writing. If these questions and others are answered in the beginning, problems may be avoided later.

Partners

Others, besides friends and family, may be interested in entering into the business with you. These could be business acquaintances, classmates, or simply entrepreneurs looking for a Business opportunity. Forming a partnership with one or more of these interested parties could be the way to fulfill not only your capital requirements but your personnel needs as well. Remember, though, that in so doing you dilute your ownership and lessen the magnitude of your control.

Shareholders

Selling shares of stock in a business as a means of raising capital is an option permitted only to Corporations. Should you decide to do so, you must first incorporate. Since this involves obtaining a corporate charter from the state in which your business will be based, it is advisable   to consult an attorney for assistance in this matter.

Offsetting the red tape inherent in forming a corporation is the corporation's unique ability to accumulate large sums of capital. Aided by such features as limited liability and easy transfer of stock ownership, the corporate is able to draw on the resources of a vast and diverse pool of investors. Brought together by a common goal-to make a profit- these investors, as shareholders, will have the right to influence corporate policy decisions. However, you can retain control by holding onto a majority of the shares of stock.

Bondholders

In addition to selling stock, corporations are permitted to sell bonds. Unlike shares of stock, which represent ownership in the business, bonds represent debt. In exchange for investing in bonds, bondholders are paid a predetermined interest rate over the life of the bond. This interest differs from dividends in that it is categorized as a business expense and therefore is deductible. When the bond matures (usually in 10 to 30 years), the bondholder receives the principal investment back.

Since bonds are a form of long-term debt, they are more often used to finance major business expansion costs such as the purchase of plant and equipment. Before making the decision to sell bonds, though, it's important that you determine your corporation's future ability to pay the annual interest and retire the bonds when they reach maturity.

Furthermore, during the early stages of your business, investors may be understandably reluctant to purchase the corporation's bonds, preferring that you establish yourself first.

Credit Unions

Credit unions generally offer lower interest rates than bunks. But to qualify for a loan, you must be a member. If you don't belong to a credit union, you might want to explore the possibility of joining one. Established for the purpose of providing members with low-interest loans, credit unions are usually formed around an employer, professional organization, church, or fraternal group.

The most common types of loans credit union make are short-term consumer loans for automobiles, furniture, boats, and so on. However, you might be able to stretch these bounds to encompass furnishings for your business, equipment, or a company car. Most credit unions will lend up to $-5,000 to purchase a computer. And, if your credit rating is good, you could qualify for a personal signature loan up to $10,000.

Savings and Loan Associations

Savings and loans have traditionally focused their attention on making long-term loans to have buyers and have played only a small role in business financing. Over the years, though, more and more savings and loans have shown an increased interest in making business loans. The reason for this shift is simple. Business loans are normally repaid over a shorter time than home loans. This enables the S & Ls to recoup their money faster.

Taking this into consideration, you might want to investigate your local savings and loans to find out which ones are pro-business.

If you own you own home, there's also the possibility that a savings and loan association will give you a loan based on your equity in the home. This route should be pursed with caution, though. Mortgaging your home to obtain business capital can be risky since a business loss could put your home in jeopardy.

Online lending. Recently, online lending services such as OnDeck and Kabbage have become a popular alternative to traditional business loans. Online lenders have the advantage of speed: An application takes only up to an hour to complete, and a decision and the accompanying fundscan be issued within days. In contrast, the traditional loan process can take weeks, or even months, to complete. Because of this, former U.S. Treasury Secretary Larry Summers said at the 2015 Lend It conference that he expects online lenders to eventually reach more than 70 percent of small businesses.

Factoring/invoice advances. Don't want to take out a loan? Services like factoring and invoice advancing may help ease growing pains for small businesses. Through this process, a service provider will front you the money on invoices that have been billed out, which you then pay back once the customer has settled its bill. Eyal Shinar, CEO of small business cash flow management company Fundbox, says these advances allow companies to close the pay gap between billed work and payments to suppliers and contractees.

"By closing the pay gap, companies can accept new projects more quickly," Shinar told Business News Daily. "Our goal is to help business owners grow their businesses and hire new workers by ensuring steady cash flow."

Product presales. Selling your products before they launch is an often-overlooked and highly effective way to raise the money needed for financing your business. Entrepreneur, Priska Diaz, was able to raise $50,000 for her company Bittylab with a presale of her Bare air-free baby bottles. The money Diaz was able to raise helped her pay for inventory, and also helped to open some doors in retail and learn about her website's visitors. Though Diaz was able to benefit greatly from this means of financing, there were still some difficulties to overcome.

"The biggest challenge was in coordinating the inventory delivery times from our supplier so that we could start fulfilling orders," Diaz said. "Another challenge was forecasting the number of units we were going to presell, resulting in a shortage. We've now passed the presale stage and sold more than originally anticipated, resulting in back orders."

Side business. New business owners can try "double-dipping" as a means of funding their startup. Entrepreneur Alex Genadinik used his revenue from tours he organized on ComeHike.com to launch Problemio.com, which builds mobile apps for planning and starting a business. After receiving donations for some of the free hikes he led, Genadinik began to charge for events, where he marketed his new site to hikers.

"I tried everything else before that, including monetizing with ads and becoming an affiliate reseller for outdoor gear, but it didn't quite work," Genadinik said. "This allowed me to work on my project without the distraction of looking for investors."

Home equity loan. For homeowners who have equity—the home's value minus what you owe— home equity loan is a great option for financing a small business. These loans generally offer interest rates that are both flexible and lower than traditional commercial rates.

"Home equity loans are very cheap, rate-wise," said Al Engel, executive vice president of consumer lending at Valley National Bank. "It is a low-cost form of borrowing that is very controllable by the entrepreneur as far as when he pays funds and redraws funds. The flexibility is tremendous. The risk is, you are putting your home on the line. If the business fails, or you fail to maintain the terms and conditions of the home equity loan or line, you risk foreclosure."

Selling assets. Sometimes, you may have a financing method and not even realize it at first. That was the case for entrepreneur Hamid Saify, who was able to fund his opinion-sharing community, ChoicePunch, by selling a car he had wanted to pass along to his children. Though it was a tough decision, Saify was able to make $30,000 from the sale of the car. That money, in turn, went toward some very important aspects of the fledgling start up.

"I used some of that money to help with the last payments to our design and development contractors," Saify said. "The rest I put into our account and used to help support marketing during our beta launch months."

Credit cards. Business credit cards are among the most readily available ways to finance a start up, and can be a quick way to get your business up and running.

"One of the few advantages is that the minimum payment on a credit card is very low," said Ken Nickel, senior vice president of community lending at Valley National Bank. "If you are a new business who is just starting out and you don't have a lot of money coming in, or you don't have a ton of expenses, you can put it on a credit card and pay the minimum payment."

However, there are some serious drawbacks to consider before using plastic to fund your startup, Nickel said. If a new business gets started and then has trouble making the payments, the interest rates and costs on the cards can build very quickly, and carrying that debt can be detrimental to a business owner's credit.

Angel investors. Those looking to finance their business can always look to an angel —an angel investor, that is. Angel investors have helped to start up many prominent companies, including Google, Yahoo and Costco. This alternative form of investing generally occurs in a company's early stages of growth, with investors expecting a 20 to 25 percent return on their investment.

"The principal advantage of an angel investor is generally that you have a friendlier atmosphere and a quicker decision-making circumstance for a smaller amount of [money]," said Mark DiSalvo, CEO of private equity fund provider Semaphore. "You are likely to get an investor who has strategic experience, so they can provide tactical benefit to the company they are investing in."

Venture capitalists. For small businesses that are beyond the start-up phase and already have revenues coming in, a venture capital investment may be appropriate. Fast-growth companies with an exit strategy already in place can gain up to tens of millions of dollars that can be used to invest, network and grow their company quickly.

Brian Haughey, assistant professor of finance and director of the investment center at Marist College, said that because venture capitalists focus on specific industries, they can generally offer advice to the entrepreneur on whether the product is going to fly or what they need to do to bring it to market. However, venture capitalists have a short leash when it comes to company loyalty and often look to recover their investment within a three- to five-year time window.

"They have to make a return and usually have a five-year time horizon," Haughey said. "If you have a product that is taking longer than that to get to market, then venture-capital investors may not be very interested in you."

Crowdfunding. Crowdfunding on websites like Kickstarter and Indiegogo can give a big boost to the financing aspirations of small businesses. These sites allow businesses to pool small investments from a number of investors instead of forcing companies to look for a single investment. Many sites allow companies to raise money in exchange for rewards or products. Others have an equity-based model in which businesses give up a bit of their share.

Before choosing a crowdfunding platform, be sure to read all the fine print and know what you're getting into. Certain sites require businesses to raise their full stated goal in order to keep any money raised on the platform. Other sites will allow companies to keep any money they raise. Additionally, sites can claim a percentage of any money raised on the site. Sites often also charge a payment-processing fee for money raised.

Grants. If your business focuses on a scientific or research-oriented field, grants from the government may be able to help fund your company. The SBA offers grants through the Small Business Innovation Research (SBIR) and the Small Business Technology Transfer (STTR) programs. Grant recipients are required to meet federal research and development goals, and to have a high potential for commercialization.

Shinar said there are not many downsides to a truly no-strings-attached grant. However, you should carefully read the fine print because grants may require that you give up part of the IT or other intellectual property, Shinar noted. Grants also can be time-consuming, and depending on the sector, the ratio of time expenditure to the odds of payout may be too high. Nonetheless, if your company could be eligible, it is wise to review the options. You might consider hiring a professional grant writer, who is familiar with the websites, the data bases, and the particular language that is necessary to successfully obtain a grant.

How Social Media Can Help Your Small Business Get Loans

The omnipresence of social media now extends beyond simple social networking, communication, and marketing. Recently, social media has been a determinate in the selection process for factoring firms and loan-givers.

The majority of online and traditional lenders view a healthy social media as a sign of a healthy, flourishing small business. The more popular that you are online, the easier it will be for them to trust you and consider you legitimate.

Aside from seeing the level of client's customer service, lenders can use social media to check up on their reputations by seeing the public's feedback and reviews. Naturally, people take to social media if they are overwhelmingly satisfied or upset with the quality of a small business's service and professionalism. Hence, it is only logical that lenders check how the general populous thinks of a small business. It is essential to exhibit a professional, courteous and service-oriented persona online.

Lastly, a savvy social media campaign can help your business get top-notch loans in that a developed presence on Facebook and Twitter makes your organization seem like an expert in its field. In other words, it allows your company to "talk the talk," so to speak. If done properly, lenders are going to assume that your business can also walk the walk, and they will therefore trust that you are worthy of favorable loans. A solid Facebook and Twitter profile is a must for small businesses seeking loans.

Precautions and Next Steps

While the plethora of lending options may make it easier than ever to get started, responsible business owners should ask themselves how much financial assistance they really need. Companies that receive more income than they truly need should be prudent in how it is used. Shinar urged such companies to make — and stick to — a disciplined budget. "It's hard to go back later and try to exert fiscal discipline," Shinar said. "It's better to start from the beginning with good corporate governance." Companies that have received a large cash infusion may benefit from bringing in an experienced partner or board member to help ensure accountability, Shinar added. As an alternative, bootstrapping your company — building it with existing resources and earned revenue — offers companies a low-risk way to test out their product. If you and your partners are able to work toward creating a functional product in your spare time, you may be able to begin to sell that product with minimal or no cash. "The advantage of bootstrapping is that you stay the boss," Shinar said. "More importantly, you get relatively quick validation from the market about whether you have a good business plan. Bootstrapping helps imbue a company with operational discipline." Owners who bootstrap retain exclusive control over their company for a longer time, allowing them to better influence its culture and goals. As your company grows, funds can be put directly back into enhancing the business, rather than into servicing your loans. In addition, they avoid less-than-favorable conditions and terms that might be imposed by lenders or additional partners. If you bootstrap, however, be prepared and open-minded about moving to the next step. If you remain without external funding for too long, you may be unable to take advantage of market opportunities. Moreover, you risk creating a business that has failed to integrate more experienced minds.

"At a certain point, you need smart partners around the table, and those partners are commonly investors," Shinar said. "If you want to grow really fast, you probably need outside sources of capital. And if you are only bootstrapping, you are missing some of the advantages of corporate governance. You may also miss some lifestyle advantage — you can go on bootstrapping for years without making money. So taking on debt may actually mean that your company can move forward." - See more at: http://www.businessnewsdaily.com/1733-small-business-financing-options-.html#sthash.uulfgViG.dpuf

CHAPTER EIGHT

How Can You Use the Small Business Administration?

The Small Business Administration (SBA) is a federal agency, created in 1953 to provide businesses with both advice and financial aid. In this regard, it can make either direct or indirect loans to businesses. A direct loan is one made by the SBA itself. An indirect loan is a loan mode by another lending institution, but guaranteed up to 90 percent by the SBA. Both kinds have lower interest rates and longer maturities than those associated with conventional loans. But, the SBA is not in competition with the financial community.

Calling itself-the "lender of last resort," the SBA usually works in partnership with lending institutions, making or guaranteeing loans only when other financing isn't available.

In granting loans, the SBA is influenced favorably by the following conditions: The business to be financed is the primary source of income for the family.

Financial assistance is not otherwise available on reasonable terms from private sources.

A reasonable amount is at stake in the venture. Generally, SBA will want at least 20 percent at stake in a start-up operation.

There is reasonable assurance or repayment.

The new venture is feasible and sound.

The applicant is of good character.

The borrower agrees not to discriminate in the business on grounds of race, creed, color, or national origin.

The applicant has ability and experience in the area of the business.

Before you attempt to put together a loan application package by yourself the SBA suggests that you prepare and collect the following information:

- A Business plan.

- A Personal financial statement.

- A Statement of personal history.

- Your Start-up costs.

- A Forecast of profit or loss.

Once you have gathered this information, you should contact your local SBA field office to discuss your business plans further. At that point, you will receive advice regarding your proposal and the preparation of a loan package.

SBA BUSINESS PLAN QUESTIONNAIRE

- The SBA will ask you the following questions as part of their financing procedure:

- Business experience and education?

- Kind of business?

- Construction, manufacturing, service, etc.

- What is your product? Describe the product or service your plan to make or sell.

- Why did you choose this kind of business?

- Sole proprietorship, partnership, or corporation?

- Amount of loan required and anticipated use offends?

- Where will the business be located?

- Why was this location selected?

- How much capital do you have and what will be invested in the business?

- Have you attended an SBA Pre-Business Workshop?

- Do you have an accountant or bookkeeping service in mind to set up financial records?

- What kinds of licensing will you require?

- How many employees will you need?

- What kind of insurance will you carry?

CONCLUSION

As you see, obtaining business loans, investors, or raising capital yourself may not only help your small business get started, but could help it stay open and possibly thrive.

But you must be armed with knowledge. Weigh the risks and the pros and cons for your business as to the different types of ways you can fund your idea, your enterprise, your dream.

Owning a business is as much a part of the American Dream as owning your own home.

With the Internet and social media, the chances for success in business are much greater than in the past. Since the 2008 recession, small businesses have helped fuel the economy's resurgence, namely through job creations. Wouldn't you like to be part of this revolution, as well as see your dream become a reality?

Read this book every day and prepare yourself with knowledge, then take action.

www.ingramcontent.com/pod-product-compliance
Lightning Source LLC
Chambersburg PA
CBHW070411190526
45169CB00003B/1207